ADAM SMITH

A pioneer of modern economics

Written by Christophe Speth
In collaboration with Brigitte Feys
Translated by Carly Probert

Business | 50MINUTES.com

ADAM SMITH

KEY INFORMATION

- **Name:** Adam Smith.
- **Born:** Kirkcaldy (Scotland) in 1723.
- **Died:** Edinburgh in 1790.
- **Context and background:** Adam Smith lived at the same time as the Industrial Revolution in the United Kingdom and the American Revolution, which brought about many socio-economic changes. He is generally considered to be the leading thinker of classical economics, the principles of which are based on liberalism.
- **Notable works:**
  - *The Theory of Moral Sentiments*, 1759.
  - *An Inquiry into the Nature and Causes of the Wealth of Nations*, 1776.
  - *Lectures on Jurisprudence*, Glasgow Edition, 1976.
  - *Works and Correspondence of Adam Smith*, Glasgow Edition, 1976.
- **Key concepts:**
  - <u>Absolute advantage:</u> Smith supported the idea that each country should specialise in the production of goods for which its productivity is higher than that of its trading partners.
  - <u>Division of labour:</u> According to Smith, the specialisation of each worker in a specific task leads to significant productivity gains.
  - <u>Invisible hand:</u> Smith believed that the market economy allows individuals to reconcile their individual interests with the public interest, and that it supports

a self-regulating economic process that allows each person to meet their own needs while serving the common good.

INTRODUCTION

Adam Smith is widely – although not universally – regarded as the father of modern economics. He was, however, influenced by many other philosophers, including the Physiocrats, who advocated a natural and free economy without state intervention. Furthermore, the Industrial Revolution had a decisive impact on the writing of *The Wealth of Nations*. For example, in this book Smith examines in detail the example of the production of pins in a factory.

Smith was a true leader, and his ideas had a lasting impact on the thinking of most of the economists who followed him, especially the classical economists who he is often mentioned alongside.

<u>DID YOU KNOW?</u>

Economists are generally divided into different categories, depending on their school of thought. From a conceptual point of view, the classical economists share the belief that the exchange value of goods reflects the cost of labour necessary for their production. In this sense, they are very different from their predecessors (the Physiocrats, who thought that value was derived solely from the exploitation of natural resources) and their successors (neoclassical economists, who

thought that value reflected the utility derived by indi-
viduals from the consumption of a good). The classical trend emerged at the start of the Industrial Revolution. However, since the late 19th century, neoclassical economists have predominated. They adopted a very different methodological approach and used mathematics extensively, whereas classical economists were content to use logical reasoning. This had the effect of making the economic theory comprehensible to a very limited audience.

David Ricardo (English economist, 1772-1823) drew on Smith's ideas to develop his theory of comparative advantage (the principle that it is in every country's interests to specialise in the production of the goods which have the lowest opportunity cost), which he would later use as a Member of Parliament to oppose protectionism. Even Karl Marx (1818-1883) – known for his anti-liberal ideology – was influenced by Adam Smith. In fact, both men shared the idea that labour is the source of value.

BIOGRAPHY

Adam Smith grew up in the peaceful Scottish countryside until the age of 14. He then discovered city life during his time at the University of Glasgow from 1737 to 1740, before complying with his family's wishes and enrolling at the University of Oxford in 1740 in order to pursue an ecclesiastical career. However, he subsequently decided to change vocation and returned to live with his mother at the age of 23, putting him in a somewhat delicate situation with no real prospects beyond his dream of obtaining an academic post at the University of Glasgow.

A fortunate encounter then convinced him to settle in Edinburgh to give public lectures. Their success certainly contributed to the realisation of his dream – which had previously seemed out of reach – of teaching at the University of Glasgow, where he lectured on logic and later, moral philosophy. It was at this time that he wrote and published *The Theory of Moral Sentiments* (1759), which contains philosophical reflections.

In 1764, after a 13-year academic career, he became the private tutor of a young English duke, Henry Scott (Duke of Buccleuch, 1746-1813). He took advantage of the opportunity to spend over two years travelling across Europe. On returning to Britain, he began working on his other great book, which is considered to be the founding text of 'modern' political economics in the 18th century, *An Inquiry into the Nature and Causes of the Wealth of Nations* (1776). He spent the last part of his life as a commissioner of customs in Edinburgh, like his father before him.

CHILDHOOD (1723-1737)

Smith was born in Kirkcaldy, a Scottish village north of Edinburgh, in 1723. He was named after his father, who died shortly before he was born. He was raised by his mother, and remained very fond of her throughout his life. The first major incident of his childhood was his abduction by gypsies when he was only two or three years old. Fortunately, the event had a happy ending, as the kidnappers were arrested when trying to get away.

Later, Smith was educated at the Burgh School of Kirkcaldy, where he soon adopted a number of somewhat strange behaviours: he talked to himself and spent his break times studying while his classmates played. Although he was particularly absent-minded by nature, he nevertheless impressed his classmates with his excellent memory and very acute sense of observation.

STUDYING AT GLASGOW (1737-1740) AND OXFORD (1740-1746)

In 1737, when he was only 14 years old, Smith left the village school to attend the University of Glasgow, which was considered relatively liberal and independent of the clergy at the time. He greatly appreciated this academic environment and would be influenced for the rest of his life by the educator and philosopher Francis Hutcheson (1694-1746), one of the founders of the Enlightenment movement in

Scotland. However, this state of intellectual grace only lasted three years.

In compliance with his family's wishes and after obtaining a scholarship in 1740, he decided to devote himself to the Church and enrolled at the University of Oxford. However, Oxford was still very conservative at this time. Contrary to what might be expected, Smith adapted relatively well to this environment and took the opportunity to learn about everything, except what he was asked. While he was supposed to spend his time studying theology, the young student made a point of deepening his knowledge in literature, physics and mathematics. He also worked on perfecting his Greek. His teachers, who were not impressed with his lack of interest in theology, brought this home to him in a famous incident. One day, when Smith was caught reading *A Treatise of Human Nature*, a three-volume work by David Hume (Scottish philosopher, 1711-1776) which was regarded as heretical, his book was confiscated and although he escaped expulsion, he was punished and made an example of. Soon after, he left Oxford, tired of his lack of freedom there.

RETURNING TO KIRKCALDY AND INTELLECTUAL RISE (1746-1764)

When he returned to his hometown of Kirkcaldy in 1746, his situation was initially difficult, marked by the lack of security that was typical for writers at that time. In 1748, two years after his return to Scotland, Smith met Lord Kames (real name Henry Home, judge and philosopher, 1696-1782), who suggested that he move to Edinburgh and give public lectures there. Smith accepted the proposal of this renowned judge, which, given the success of his lectures and the ever-growing audience they attracted, accelerated his rise in the intellectual world. At this time, he also met the man who later became his best friend, David Hume. In 1751, he joined the University of Glasgow and lectured in logic, then moral philosophy; later, in 1787, he was given the honorary position of Lord Rector of the university. He published *The Theory of Moral Sentiments* in 1759, a work that was immensely successful in England as well as Scotland.

Smith had by now developed a very good reputation, and he was soon asked to coordinate the education of a young duke. He turned down the offer and decided to dedicate himself to studying law and economics, as he had been previously only studied morality. In 1763, the offer was repeated, and this time Smith agreed to take over the young man's education.

THE JOURNEY TO FRANCE (1764-1766)

As was customary at that time, a great trip was taken to make the education of Henry Scott, Duke of Buccleuch, the best it could possibly be, and Smith and his student left for France in the spring of 1764. Following a brief stay in Paris, they both went to Toulouse, where Smith worked on numerous pieces of research and, some say, began writing *The Wealth of Nations*. After around 15 months in Toulouse, Scott and Smith settled in Geneva for two months. They then returned to Paris to end their continental travels. There, Smith met the Physiocrat François Quesnay (1694-1774), from whom he drew considerable inspiration when writing *The Wealth of Nations*. The student and teacher finally returned to London in the autumn of 1766, after a journey lasting around 30 months.

WRITING *THE WEALTH OF NATIONS* (1766-1776) AND A CAREER IN CUSTOMS (1778-1790)

Back in Kirkcaldy, Smith devoted himself entirely to writing *An Inquiry into the Nature and Causes of the Wealth of Nations*. Some think he wanted to publish something even bigger, including in particular a critical study of the history of law. Letters written by Smith requesting documents from Lord Hailes (real name David Dalrymple, Scottish judge, 1726-1792) seem to support with this thesis. However, Smith decided at some point to focus on the study of economic mechanisms. To concentrate fully on his new writing project, he chose to isolate himself: apart from a trip from Edinburgh to London in 1773, he remained in his hometown without interruption until his book was published. His friend David Hume repeatedly complained to him about this self-imposed isolation and offered to join him when passing near Kirkcaldy. Smith refused, and his isolation seemed to serve him well: *An Inquiry into the Nature and Causes of the Wealth of Nations* received an enthusiastic reception when it was published in 1776. Spurred on by his growing prestige, Smith moved to London for two years.

In 1778, he became a commissioner of customs in Edinburgh, a position that he held until his death in 1790.

Smith's contemporaries – great thinkers of the Enlightenment

In France, the Enlightenment period – the 18th century – brought new ideas from thinkers such as:

- the Enlightenment writers Voltaire (1694-1778) and Montesquieu (1689-1755);
- François Quesnay (1694-1774), encyclopedist and leader of the school of Physiocrats;
- Jean-Baptiste Say (1767-1832), a classical liberal economist who wrote *A Treatise on Political Economy* (1803) and popularised the law of markets, known as Say's Law;
- Jacques Necker (1732-1804), finance minister under Louis XVI, who published successful essays on economic policy;
- Anne Robert Jacques Turgot (1727-1781), the Controller-General of Finances under Louis XVI, who supported Smith's invisible hand theory.

In Germany, Karl Marx (1818-1883) opposed emerging capitalism and published his own political and economic critique of society.

In Britain, there were the great Scottish thinkers of the Enlightenment David Hume (1711-1776) and Thomas Reid (1710-1776), as well as economists such as David Ricardo (1772-1823) and John Stuart Mill (1806-1873), a follower of Hume and proponent of utilitarianism.

Economics throughout history

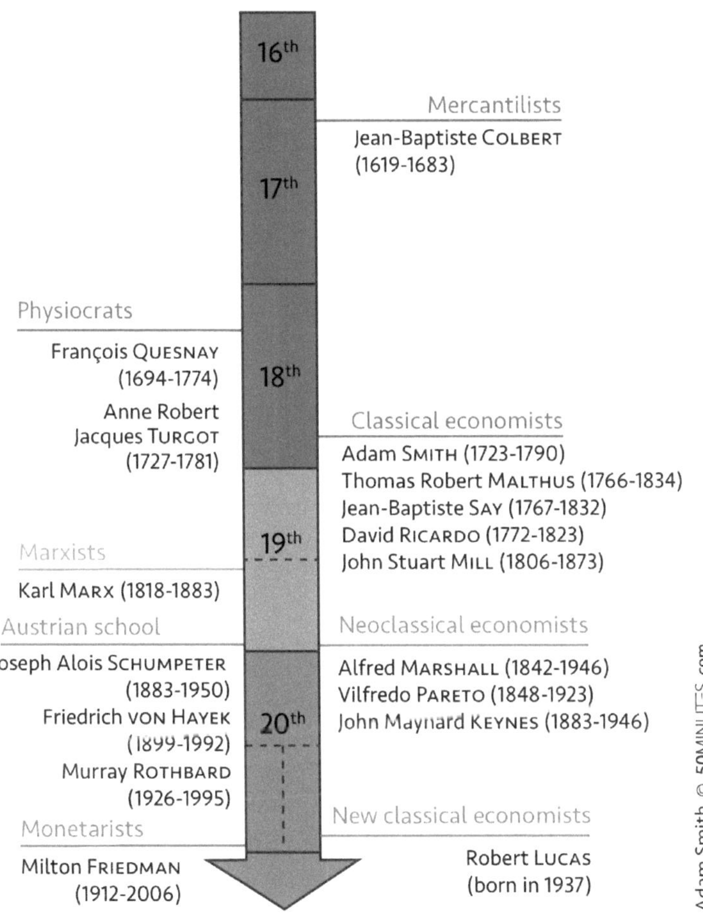

KEY WORKS

Adam Smith was a philosopher before he was an economist. Like most intellectuals of his time, he saw economics as a branch of philosophy, alongside morality, politics and law. Smith was therefore the archetype of the honest man who is interested in all disciplines. For this reason, it is worth beginning by examining *The Theory of Moral Sentiments*: although this work does not deal with economics, it enables us to better appreciate his final masterpiece, *The Wealth of Nations*.

THE THEORY OF MORAL SENTIMENTS (1759)

In this book, Smith tries to explain a paradox: even if there is nothing good about man, he nonetheless has the ability to make moral judgments or to judge himself, as he has the ability to become an observer and take a step back from himself.

In this way, he questioned the cause of ambition and vanity in human beings. According to Smith, some look to increase their power and wealth not to improve their well-being, but to attract the attention of others. The real suffering of the poor is therefore the fact that they receive only indifference while the rich enjoy constant attention:

> "A stranger to human nature, who saw the indifference of men about the misery of their inferiors, and the regret and indignation which they feel for the misfortunes and sufferings of those above them, would be apt to imagine, that pain must be more agonizing, and the convulsions of

> death more terrible to persons of higher rank, than to those
> of meaner stations." (Smith, 2012: 50)

Smith also highlights the nature of the qualities needed to reach a high social rank. While the wealthy can merely flaunt their sophisticated education, the disadvantaged must demonstrate unmatched entrepreneurial spirit.

According to Smith, what really motivates humans to desire wealth is:

- The fact that they want to become increasingly rich in order to attract the attention of others;
- The fact that wealth allows them to acquire some higher-quality items, which they think will increase their level of wellbeing. Their interest in these objects is therefore not linked to their wellbeing that actually results from them.

Smith explains the possession of "trinkets of frivolous utility" using a parable about a young businessman with boundless ambition (Smith, 2012: 179-180), and is surprised by the amount of energy invested in the search for such objects.

Although Smith criticises such behaviour as a moralist, he nonetheless sees it as conducive to social harmony:

> "And it is well that nature imposes upon us in this manner. It
> is this deception which rouses and keeps in continual motion
> the industry of mankind." (Smith, 2012: 181)

The concept of sympathy is fundamental in *The Theory of Moral Sentiments*, since it is through this that Smith explains judgments on propriety and merit. It can be defined as an individual's ability to imagine themselves in the place of another. In a way, it involves living other people's lives by proxy: even if we are not in their situation, we imagine ourselves in their place and share their feelings. As such, each of us desires the greatest happiness for the greatest number of people possible.

After explaining the nature of judgments made by individuals about others, Smith demonstrates how man can form such judgments about himself. As these judgments take the form of an obligation, these generally lead to appropriate and praiseworthy behaviour. The author introduces the concept of the impartial spectator to illustrate the workings of this process of reflexive sympathy. This concept involves judging an action from a different point of view to that of the person who performed it or is affected by it. The author thinks that our mind constantly makes its moral judgment by taking a step back and adopting the stance of the independent spectator.

Despite his belief that we are guided by ambition, Smith qualified his remarks and said that an impartial spectator – our conscience – can be found in each of us, which prevents us from harming others and which pushes us, in certain circumstances, to be generous. According to him, the real motive for this behaviour is not altruistic concern for the wellbeing of others, but the fear of not acting in accordance with our conscience:

> "It is not the love of our neighbour, it is not the love of mankind, which upon many occasions prompts us to the practice of those divine virtues. It is a stronger love, a more powerful affection, which generally takes place upon such occasions; the love of what is honourable and noble, of the grandeur, and dignity, and superiority of our own characters." (Smith 2012: 133)

Smith illustrates his argument by imagining the hypothetical reaction of Europeans to an earthquake in China. According to him, such a disaster would have no effect on our conscience because we know that it is not our fault. At most, we would discuss it at the time, but all would be forgotten soon after. This attitude is described with great clarity in the book (Smith, 2012: 132) and is still relevant today.

AN INQUIRY INTO THE NATURE AND CAUSES OF THE WEALTH OF NATIONS (1776)

This book, undoubtedly Smith's most famous work, is often considered to have revolutionised economic policy in England. The three main themes it deals with are:

- the division of labour, which enables the distribution of tasks and the specialisation of workers;
- the fixing of prices, both on the goods and services mar-

ket and on the labour market;

- the extent of the role of the state in managing the country's economy.

Division of labour

One of the central theses of *The Wealth of Nations* is that the division of labour is at the root of wealth creation. According to Smith, the specialisation of workers allows them to be more productive, for several reasons:

- firstly, when the same task is repeated often, it can be executed more quickly (this is what allows us to gain an absolute advantage in producing a good);
- next, the fact of having only one activity saves transition time between different tasks;
- finally, Smith believed that the division of labour was responsible for the invention of many machines, which resulted in an increase in worker productivity.

That said, the division of labour has its limits. According to Smith, the scope of the market (the number of consumers it can potentially target) must be large enough for worker specialisation to be implemented. He notes that the development of maritime communication routes catalysed the division of labour by allowing industries to reach more consumers (emphasis ours):

> **"As by means of water-carriage a more extensive market is opened** to every sort of industry than what land-carriage alone can afford it, so it is upon the sea-coast, and along the banks of navigable rivers, that industry of every kind

naturally begins to **subdivide and improve itself**." (Smith, 1811: 14)

Fixing of prices

In addition to the division of labour, Smith was also interested in how prices are determined and fixed. In this, he was a precursor of what is now known as the law of supply and demand. He believed that the market price always tends towards a level that he called the natural price (this can be roughly defined as the lowest price for which a trader is willing to produce a good). Smith demonstrated his intuition as follows (Book 1, Chapter 7).

Pricing according to Adam Smith

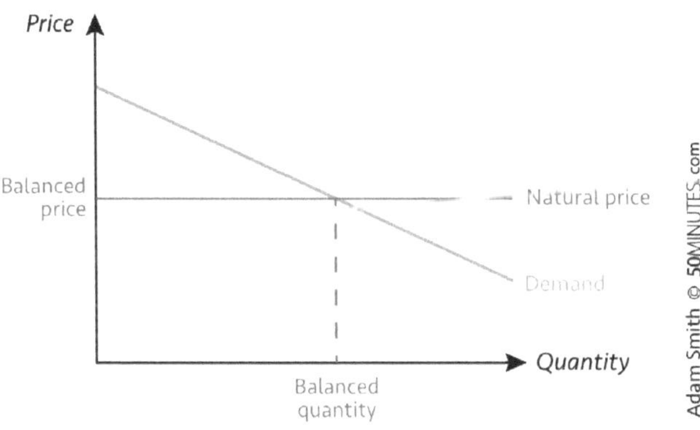

- If the market price is higher than the natural price (provided that the level of competition is sufficient), existing producers have an incentive to produce more, while new

producers will want to move into the market to enjoy a high enough profit. As the quantity produced increases, consumers no longer have to outbid one another to purchase the good in question. As a result, the market price decreases until it reaches its natural level.
- Conversely, if the market price is below the natural price, the quantity produced decreases (since producers are leaving the market) until the market price returns to its natural level.

The role of the state

Smith has a clear vision of the role of the state in managing the economy of a nation. In general, he thinks that the government should not interfere. However, he does not some exceptions (Book 4, Chapter 9 and Book 5, Chapter 1):

- the state must guarantee justice and the security of the territory, which implies a national defence and state police;
- the state must be involved in the construction and maintenance of major infrastructure (roads, canals, etc.);
- finally, the state must ensure that every citizen receives an elementary level of education.

LIMITATIONS AND EXTENSIONS

LIMITATIONS AND CRITICISMS

Division of labour

Although the principle of the division of labour put forward by Smith had initially been taken up by theorists such as Frederick Winslow Taylor (1856-1915), who pushed it to its furthest limits, it then experienced a slow decline. Taylor created a system of labour organisation that he described as 'scientific'. This is based on several basic principles:

- work is divided vertically between managers and workers (the managers think about the most efficient way to produce and workers act on their orders);
- work is divided horizontally (each worker specialises in a specific task; this was the beginnings of the production line);
- to encourage workers to be a fast as possible, Taylor suggested paying them according to their performance.

These ideas had an incredible impact in developed countries throughout the 20th century. Fordism – an extension of Taylorism – also experienced its peak during the 30 years of rapid economic growth in developed countries following the Second World War. However, recent technological advances (the automatisation of increasingly complex chains) and the improved level of education over generations have contributed to the virtual disappearance of the production line. Work has perhaps become very specialised in intellectual terms, but the tasks performed manually have tended to become more varied.

Smith's contributions

Some believe that Smith is in no way an original author, and should not be identified as the father of economics. Murray Rothbard (1926-1995) strongly criticised Smith, accusing him of plagiarism, and even worse, of taking the ideas he plagiarised in the wrong direction (Rothbard, 2006). According to Rothbard, economics actually dates from the Middle Ages; in this way, his work challenged a widely-held idea about economics.

An analysis limited to the context of its time

As he was one of the first modern economists, Adam Smith only laid the foundations for a new and rapidly developing science. As such, his analysis was limited to the context of its time, which could not imagine or anticipate the changes that would occur in our modern world two centuries later. For example, Smith did not seem to realise the importance of externalities. Later, economists considered this fundamental principle and described two forms of it:

- Negative externalities can be defined as the behaviour of an individual that has a negative impact on another individual. The classic example is air pollution.
- Positive externalities can be defined as the behaviour of an individual that has a positive impact on another individual. The classic example is education.

Controversies

While Smith considers that the search for exchange is a characteristic unique to humans, the Hungarian intellectual Karl Polanyi (1886-1964) challenges this view in his book *The Great Transformation: The Political and Economic Origins of Our Time* (1944), a classic work which experienced a revival after the economic crisis of 2008. Polanyi illustrates his argument with specific examples. In Chapter 4, he discusses the organisation of certain primitive societies, which are based on reciprocity and redistribution by a leader, rather than exchange. These societies are often self-sufficient and powerful social control still remains.

Beyond this positive criticism, there is also a normative criticism of Smith, and of classical and neoclassical economists more generally. Even today, it is often said that economic science neglects social bonds. This criticism seems apt insofar as the market makes economic relations increasingly anonymous. However, other criticisms of economists seem much less justified. The best example of this is their attitude towards the environmental problem. Economists generally agree on the need to tax polluters or set up a market for pollution licences to fight against the emission of greenhouse gases. This means leaving the market to do its work, before letting the state correct any remaining imperfections. This can be seen as a legacy of Smith's ideas, as he thought that the state should intervene in government functions, investment in major projects and the education of young people.

RELATED MODELS AND EXTENSIONS

Ricardo's comparative advantage

As we have seen in the section about *The Wealth of Nations*, the concept of absolute advantage concept developed by Smith was subsequently extended with Ricardo's concept of comparative advantage.

WHAT IS THE DIFFERENCE BETWEEN ABSOLUTE ADVANTAGE AND COMPARATIVE ADVANTAGE?

Economists often distinguish between the concepts of absolute advantage and comparative advantage. The former was developed by Smith, who put forward the idea that it is in the interests of two countries (or two individuals) to exchange two goods if each country has an absolute advantage – i.e. they can produce at a lower cost – in the production of one of the two goods. However, this view does not take into account the options of a country that can produce both products at lower costs than its neighbour.

David Ricardo extended the theory of absolute advantage for such situations. A British man from a family of Portuguese origin, he used the example of the trade in wine and cloth between England and Portugal: according to him, it is in the interests of each country to specialise in the production of the good for which they have a comparative advantage, meaning the good with the largest absolute advantage (for the country capable of producing both goods at a lowest cost) or the lowest absolute disadvantage (for the country with no absolute advantage in the production of either good). As such, even the country that holds the absolute advantage in both goods benefits from exchange, as this saves work.

The theories of Smith and Ricardo, although different, both justify international trade. Both men – especially Ricardo as an MP – also vigorously opposed protectionism.

The theory of value

With regard to the theory of value, the classical economists are opposed to their neoclassical counterparts. As a reminder, Smith, Ricardo and Marx believed that the exchange value of a good depended on the work necessary to produce it.

Conversely, neoclassical economists based the value of a good on its marginal utility (the utility of consumption of an additional unit of that good). The two theories seem to complement one another in a way. Alfred Marshall (English economist, 1842-1924) believed that in the short term, the neoclassical economists were correct (prices adjust, but not the quantities produced, which means that demand reacts more quickly than supply to a crisis) while in the long term, classical reasoning seems most apt (the quantity produced also adjusts).

SUMMARY

- Adam Smith, considered to be the founder of modern economics in the 18th century, was a philosopher before becoming an economist, which encouraged him to understand the world as a whole: emphasis on the importance of the division of labour, the beginnings of the law of supply and demand, etc.
- Living at a time when the Enlightenment encouraged scientific exchange and rivalry, Smith met Voltaire, Quesnay and Hume, among others. Hume would later become his best friend.
- His work, known for its consistency, gave subsequent economists a lot to think about. Many of his ideas are still studied and discussed in the light of contemporary socioeconomic issues, including the globalisation of markets.
  - In *The Theory of Moral Sentiments*, Smith used moral philosophy to analyse human behaviour.
  - In *The Wealth of Nations*, Smith laid many of the bases of economic science.
- From an ideological point of view, Smith was a liberal. He believed that state intervention should be limited to government functions (justice, defence and police). There were two exceptions to this: infrastructure and education.
- Smith was aware that the development of maritime transport played a major role in economic growth by allowing for a greater division of labour.
- He and Ricardo opposed any form of protectionism. To

justify their views, they developed the theories of absolute advantage and comparative advantage respectively.

- Smith inspired many economists: Ricardo, Say and Marx are probably the best known of them, and are all part of the classical school, although Marx is situated somewhat on the fringes. Neoclassical economists were also inspired by him, but to a lesser extent.
- Nonetheless, Smith's ideas met with a number of criticisms. In particular, his theory of absolute advantage does not take into account situations where a country is more productive that another country in all sectors. In addition, his theory of value underestimates the role of short-term demand.

FURTHER READING

BIBLIOGRAPHY

- Alternatives Économiques (2005) *Adam Smith (1723-1790).* [Online]. [Accessed 4 July 2014]. Available from: <http://www.alternatives-economiques.fr/adam-smith--1723-1790-_fr_art_222_27861.html>
- Andlil (2013) *Adam Smith.* [Online]. [Accessed 4 July 2014]. Available from: <http://www.andlil.com/adam-smith-128211.html>
- Andlil (2013) *Théorie de l'économie classique.* [Online]. [Accessed 4 July 2014]. Available from: <http://www.andlil.com/theorie-de-leconomie-classique-151943.html>
- Beraud, A. (1993) La contribution fondatrice. Origine et développement de la pensée économique d'Adam Smith. *Nouvelle Histoire de la pensée économique.* Volume 1, pp. 309-364.
- De Vroey, M. (2009) Les libéralismes économiques et la crise. *Revue française d'économie.* 24(2), pp. 3-37.
- Delatour, A. (1886) *Adam Smith, sa vie, ses travaux, ses doctrines.* Paris: Guillaumin.
- Diatkine, D. (1991) *Présentation de la* Richesse des nations. *Adam Smith.* Paris: GF-Flammarion. [Online]. [Accessed 4 July 2014]. Available from: <http://theme.univ-paris1.fr/M1/hpe/Diatkine_RDN.pdf>
- e-Economie (No date) *Les courants de pensée en économie.* [Online]. [Accessed 4 July 2014]. Available from: <http://www.e-economie.com/courants.php>
- Fourastié, J. (1979) *Les Trente Glorieuses ou la révolution*

invisible de 1946 à 1975. Paris: Fayard.

- Guédon, J.-M. (2009) Le lien social chez Adam Smith : le marché, la sympathie, l'État. *Ithaque*. Volume 5, pp. 101-128.
- Heilbroner, R. (1987) *The Essential Adam Smith*. New York: W.W. Norton & Company.
- Introduction à l'analyse économique (No date) *Les théories de la valeur*. [Online]. [Accessed 4 July 2014]. Available from: <http://www.pise.info/eco/valeur.htm>
- Larousse (No date) *Adam Smith*. [Online]. [Accessed 4 July 2014]. Available from: <http://www.larousse.fr/encyclopedie/personnage/Adam_Smith/144596>
- Larousse (No date) *David Ricardo*. [Online]. [Accessed 4 July 2014]. Available from: <http://www.larousse.fr/encyclopedie/personnage/David_Ricardo/140892>
- Larousse (No date) *École classique en économie*. [Online]. [Accessed 4 July 2014]. Available from: <http://www.larousse.fr/encyclopedie/divers/%C3%A9cole_classique_en_%C3%A9conomie/187107>
- Rae, J. (1895) *Life of Adam Smith*. London: Macmillan & Co.
- Rothbard, M. (2006) *Economic Thought Before Adam Smith*. Cheltenham: Edward Elgar Publishing.
- Smith, A. (2012) *The Theory of Moral Sentiments*. New York: Dover Publications, Inc.
- Smith, A. (2014) *The Wealth of Nations*. CreateSpace Independent Publishing Platform.
- Taylor, F.W. (1911) *The Principles of Scientific Management*. London: Harper & Brothers.

IMPROVE YOUR GENERAL KNOWLEDGE

IN A BLINK OF AN EYE !

www.50minutes.com